DATE:..../...../........

COUNTED BY:...

LOCATION/BRAND...

MW00934780

SKU	DESCRIPTION	QUANTITY	LOCATION	COMMENTS

DATE:..../...../.........   TIME......:.......

COUNTED BY:..

LOCATION/BRAND..

SKU	DESCRIPTION	QUANTITY	LOCATION	COMMENTS

DATE:...../...../.........   TIME......:........

COUNTED BY:...

LOCATION/BRAND...

SKU	DESCRIPTION	QUANTITY	LOCATION	COMMENTS

DATE:..../...../.........   TIME......:........

COUNTED BY:...

LOCATION/BRAND...

SKU	DESCRIPTION	QUANTITY	LOCATION	COMMENTS

DATE:..../...../........   TIME......:.......

COUNTED BY:..

LOCATION/BRAND..

SKU	DESCRIPTION	QUANTITY	LOCATION	COMMENTS

DATE:..../...../........   TIME......:........

COUNTED BY:...

LOCATION/BRAND...

SKU	DESCRIPTION	QUANTITY	LOCATION	COMMENTS

DATE:..../...../.........   TIME......:.......

COUNTED BY:..

LOCATION/BRAND..

SKU	DESCRIPTION	QUANTITY	LOCATION	COMMENTS

DATE:..../...../........   TIME......:........

COUNTED BY:...

LOCATION/BRAND...

SKU	DESCRIPTION	QUANTITY	LOCATION	COMMENTS

DATE:..../...../.........   TIME......:........

COUNTED BY:...

LOCATION/BRAND...

SKU	DESCRIPTION	QUANTITY	LOCATION	COMMENTS

DATE:..../...../.........   TIME......:........

COUNTED BY:..

LOCATION/BRAND..

SKU	DESCRIPTION	QUANTITY	LOCATION	COMMENTS

DATE:..../...../.........   TIME......:........

COUNTED BY:...

LOCATION/BRAND..

SKU	DESCRIPTION	QUANTITY	LOCATION	COMMENTS

DATE:..../...../......... TIME......:........

COUNTED BY:...

LOCATION/BRAND..

SKU	DESCRIPTION	QUANTITY	LOCATION	COMMENTS

DATE:..../...../......... TIME......:........

COUNTED BY:...

LOCATION/BRAND...

SKU	DESCRIPTION	QUANTITY	LOCATION	COMMENTS

DATE:..../...../.........   TIME......:........

COUNTED BY:...

LOCATION/BRAND...

SKU	DESCRIPTION	QUANTITY	LOCATION	COMMENTS

DATE:..../...../......... TIME......:.......

COUNTED BY:...

LOCATION/BRAND...

SKU	DESCRIPTION	QUANTITY	LOCATION	COMMENTS

DATE:..../...../.........   TIME......:........

COUNTED BY:...

LOCATION/BRAND..

SKU	DESCRIPTION	QUANTITY	LOCATION	COMMENTS

DATE:..../...../.........   TIME......:.......

COUNTED BY:...

LOCATION/BRAND..

SKU	DESCRIPTION	QUANTITY	LOCATION	COMMENTS

DATE:..../...../.........   TIME......:........

COUNTED BY:...

LOCATION/BRAND...

SKU	DESCRIPTION	QUANTITY	LOCATION	COMMENTS

DATE:...../...../......... TIME......:.......

COUNTED BY:...

LOCATION/BRAND...

SKU	DESCRIPTION	QUANTITY	LOCATION	COMMENTS

DATE:..../...../.........   TIME......:........

COUNTED BY:...

LOCATION/BRAND...

SKU	DESCRIPTION	QUANTITY	LOCATION	COMMENTS

DATE:..../...../.........   TIME......:.......

COUNTED BY:...

LOCATION/BRAND...

SKU	DESCRIPTION	QUANTITY	LOCATION	COMMENTS

DATE:..../...../.........   TIME......:........

COUNTED BY:...

LOCATION/BRAND...

SKU	DESCRIPTION	QUANTITY	LOCATION	COMMENTS

DATE:..../...../......... TIME......:........

COUNTED BY:...

LOCATION/BRAND...

SKU	DESCRIPTION	QUANTITY	LOCATION	COMMENTS

DATE:..../...../........   TIME......:........
COUNTED BY:...
LOCATION/BRAND...

SKU	DESCRIPTION	QUANTITY	LOCATION	COMMENTS

DATE:..../...../.........   TIME......:........

COUNTED BY:...

LOCATION/BRAND...

SKU	DESCRIPTION	QUANTITY	LOCATION	COMMENTS

DATE:...../...../........ TIME......:........

COUNTED BY:...

LOCATION/BRAND...

SKU	DESCRIPTION	QUANTITY	LOCATION	COMMENTS

DATE:..../..../........   TIME......:.......

COUNTED BY:...

LOCATION/BRAND...

SKU	DESCRIPTION	QUANTITY	LOCATION	COMMENTS

DATE:..../...../........   TIME......:........

COUNTED BY:..

LOCATION/BRAND...

SKU	DESCRIPTION	QUANTITY	LOCATION	COMMENTS

DATE:..../...../.........   TIME......:........

COUNTED BY:...

LOCATION/BRAND...

SKU	DESCRIPTION	QUANTITY	LOCATION	COMMENTS

DATE:..../...../.........   TIME......:........

COUNTED BY:..

LOCATION/BRAND...

SKU	DESCRIPTION	QUANTITY	LOCATION	COMMENTS

DATE:..../...../.........   TIME......:.......

COUNTED BY:..

LOCATION/BRAND..

SKU	DESCRIPTION	QUANTITY	LOCATION	COMMENTS

DATE:..../...../........ TIME......:........

COUNTED BY:..

LOCATION/BRAND..

SKU	DESCRIPTION	QUANTITY	LOCATION	COMMENTS

DATE:..../...../........   TIME......:........

COUNTED BY:...

LOCATION/BRAND..

SKU	DESCRIPTION	QUANTITY	LOCATION	COMMENTS

DATE:..../...../.........   TIME......:........

COUNTED BY:...

LOCATION/BRAND..

SKU	DESCRIPTION	QUANTITY	LOCATION	COMMENTS

DATE:..../...../........   TIME......:.......

COUNTED BY:..

LOCATION/BRAND...

SKU	DESCRIPTION	QUANTITY	LOCATION	COMMENTS

DATE:..../...../........   TIME......:.......

COUNTED BY:...

LOCATION/BRAND...

SKU	DESCRIPTION	QUANTITY	LOCATION	COMMENTS

DATE:..../...../.........   TIME......:........

COUNTED BY:...

LOCATION/BRAND..

SKU	DESCRIPTION	QUANTITY	LOCATION	COMMENTS

DATE:..../...../........   TIME......:........

COUNTED BY:..

LOCATION/BRAND..

SKU	DESCRIPTION	QUANTITY	LOCATION	COMMENTS

DATE:..../...../......... TIME......:.......

COUNTED BY:...

LOCATION/BRAND..

SKU	DESCRIPTION	QUANTITY	LOCATION	COMMENTS

DATE:..../...../........ TIME......:........

COUNTED BY:...

LOCATION/BRAND...

SKU	DESCRIPTION	QUANTITY	LOCATION	COMMENTS

DATE:..../...../.........   TIME......:........

COUNTED BY:...

LOCATION/BRAND...

SKU	DESCRIPTION	QUANTITY	LOCATION	COMMENTS

DATE:..../...../.........   TIME......:.......

COUNTED BY:...

LOCATION/BRAND...

SKU	DESCRIPTION	QUANTITY	LOCATION	COMMENTS

DATE:..../...../.........   TIME......:........

COUNTED BY:...

LOCATION/BRAND...

SKU	DESCRIPTION	QUANTITY	LOCATION	COMMENTS

DATE:..../...../.........   TIME......:.......

COUNTED BY:...

LOCATION/BRAND..

SKU	DESCRIPTION	QUANTITY	LOCATION	COMMENTS

DATE:..../...../.........   TIME......:.......

COUNTED BY:...

LOCATION/BRAND...

SKU	DESCRIPTION	QUANTITY	LOCATION	COMMENTS

DATE:..../...../........   TIME......:.......
COUNTED BY:..
LOCATION/BRAND..

SKU	DESCRIPTION	QUANTITY	LOCATION	COMMENTS

DATE:..../...../........   TIME......:........

COUNTED BY:..

LOCATION/BRAND...

SKU	DESCRIPTION	QUANTITY	LOCATION	COMMENTS

DATE:..../...../........   TIME......:........

COUNTED BY:...

LOCATION/BRAND..

SKU	DESCRIPTION	QUANTITY	LOCATION	COMMENTS

DATE:..../...../........   TIME......:........

COUNTED BY:..

LOCATION/BRAND..

SKU	DESCRIPTION	QUANTITY	LOCATION	COMMENTS

DATE:..../...../.........   TIME......:........

COUNTED BY:..

LOCATION/BRAND..

SKU	DESCRIPTION	QUANTITY	LOCATION	COMMENTS

DATE:..../...../........   TIME......:.......

COUNTED BY:...

LOCATION/BRAND...

SKU	DESCRIPTION	QUANTITY	LOCATION	COMMENTS

DATE:..../...../........   TIME......:.......

COUNTED BY:...

LOCATION/BRAND...

SKU	DESCRIPTION	QUANTITY	LOCATION	COMMENTS

DATE:..../...../.........   TIME......:.......

COUNTED BY:...

LOCATION/BRAND...

SKU	DESCRIPTION	QUANTITY	LOCATION	COMMENTS

DATE:..../...../........ TIME......:.......

COUNTED BY:...

LOCATION/BRAND...

SKU	DESCRIPTION	QUANTITY	LOCATION	COMMENTS

DATE:..../...../........   TIME......:........

COUNTED BY:...

LOCATION/BRAND..

SKU	DESCRIPTION	QUANTITY	LOCATION	COMMENTS

DATE:..../...../........   TIME......:.......

COUNTED BY:...

LOCATION/BRAND...

SKU	DESCRIPTION	QUANTITY	LOCATION	COMMENTS

DATE:..../...../.........   TIME......:........

COUNTED BY:..

LOCATION/BRAND...

SKU	DESCRIPTION	QUANTITY	LOCATION	COMMENTS

DATE:..../...../.........   TIME......:........

COUNTED BY:..

LOCATION/BRAND..

SKU	DESCRIPTION	QUANTITY	LOCATION	COMMENTS

DATE:..../...../.........   TIME......:........

COUNTED BY:...

LOCATION/BRAND...

SKU	DESCRIPTION	QUANTITY	LOCATION	COMMENTS

DATE:..../...../........   TIME......:.......

COUNTED BY:...

LOCATION/BRAND...

SKU	DESCRIPTION	QUANTITY	LOCATION	COMMENTS

DATE:..../...../........   TIME......:........

COUNTED BY:...

LOCATION/BRAND...

SKU	DESCRIPTION	QUANTITY	LOCATION	COMMENTS

DATE:..../...../........   TIME......:........

COUNTED BY:..

LOCATION/BRAND..

SKU	DESCRIPTION	QUANTITY	LOCATION	COMMENTS

DATE:..../...../.........   TIME......:........

COUNTED BY:..

LOCATION/BRAND..

SKU	DESCRIPTION	QUANTITY	LOCATION	COMMENTS

DATE:..../...../........   TIME......:........
COUNTED BY:...
LOCATION/BRAND..

SKU	DESCRIPTION	QUANTITY	LOCATION	COMMENTS

DATE:..../...../.........   TIME......:........

COUNTED BY:..

LOCATION/BRAND...

SKU	DESCRIPTION	QUANTITY	LOCATION	COMMENTS

DATE:..../...../.........   TIME......:........

COUNTED BY:...

LOCATION/BRAND...

SKU	DESCRIPTION	QUANTITY	LOCATION	COMMENTS

DATE:..../...../........   TIME......:........

COUNTED BY:...

LOCATION/BRAND...

SKU	DESCRIPTION	QUANTITY	LOCATION	COMMENTS

DATE:..../...../........   TIME......:........

COUNTED BY:...

LOCATION/BRAND...

SKU	DESCRIPTION	QUANTITY	LOCATION	COMMENTS

DATE:..../...../........   TIME......:........

COUNTED BY:...

LOCATION/BRAND..

SKU	DESCRIPTION	QUANTITY	LOCATION	COMMENTS

DATE:..../...../.........   TIME......:........

COUNTED BY:..

LOCATION/BRAND..

SKU	DESCRIPTION	QUANTITY	LOCATION	COMMENTS

DATE:..../...../......... TIME......:.......

COUNTED BY:..

LOCATION/BRAND...

SKU	DESCRIPTION	QUANTITY	LOCATION	COMMENTS

DATE:..../...../.........　　　　TIME......:........

COUNTED BY:...

LOCATION/BRAND...

SKU	DESCRIPTION	QUANTITY	LOCATION	COMMENTS

DATE:..../...../.........   TIME......:........

COUNTED BY:..

LOCATION/BRAND..

SKU	DESCRIPTION	QUANTITY	LOCATION	COMMENTS

DATE:..../...../.........   TIME......:........

COUNTED BY:..

LOCATION/BRAND...

SKU	DESCRIPTION	QUANTITY	LOCATION	COMMENTS

DATE:..../...../......... TIME......:.......

COUNTED BY:...

LOCATION/BRAND..

SKU	DESCRIPTION	QUANTITY	LOCATION	COMMENTS

DATE:..../...../.........   TIME......:.......

COUNTED BY:...

LOCATION/BRAND...

SKU	DESCRIPTION	QUANTITY	LOCATION	COMMENTS

DATE:..../...../.........   TIME......:.......

COUNTED BY:...

LOCATION/BRAND...

SKU	DESCRIPTION	QUANTITY	LOCATION	COMMENTS

DATE:..../...../........   TIME......:........

COUNTED BY:..

LOCATION/BRAND...

SKU	DESCRIPTION	QUANTITY	LOCATION	COMMENTS

DATE:..../...../.........   TIME......:.......

COUNTED BY:...

LOCATION/BRAND...

SKU	DESCRIPTION	QUANTITY	LOCATION	COMMENTS

DATE:..../...../........   TIME......:........

COUNTED BY:..

LOCATION/BRAND..

SKU	DESCRIPTION	QUANTITY	LOCATION	COMMENTS

DATE:..../...../.........   TIME......:.......

COUNTED BY:...

LOCATION/BRAND...

SKU	DESCRIPTION	QUANTITY	LOCATION	COMMENTS

DATE:..../...../........   TIME......:........
COUNTED BY:...
LOCATION/BRAND...

SKU	DESCRIPTION	QUANTITY	LOCATION	COMMENTS

DATE:..../...../........ TIME......:........

COUNTED BY:...

LOCATION/BRAND..

SKU	DESCRIPTION	QUANTITY	LOCATION	COMMENTS

DATE:..../...../........   TIME......:........

COUNTED BY:..

LOCATION/BRAND..

SKU	DESCRIPTION	QUANTITY	LOCATION	COMMENTS

DATE:..../...../.........　　　　TIME......:........

COUNTED BY:..

LOCATION/BRAND..

SKU	DESCRIPTION	QUANTITY	LOCATION	COMMENTS

DATE:..../...../.........   TIME......:.......

COUNTED BY:..

LOCATION/BRAND...

SKU	DESCRIPTION	QUANTITY	LOCATION	COMMENTS

DATE:..../..../........   TIME......:.......

COUNTED BY:...

LOCATION/BRAND...

SKU	DESCRIPTION	QUANTITY	LOCATION	COMMENTS

DATE:..../...../........　　　　TIME......:.......

COUNTED BY:...

LOCATION/BRAND...

SKU	DESCRIPTION	QUANTITY	LOCATION	COMMENTS

DATE:..../...../........   TIME......:.......

COUNTED BY:...

LOCATION/BRAND..

SKU	DESCRIPTION	QUANTITY	LOCATION	COMMENTS

DATE:..../...../........   TIME......:........

COUNTED BY:...

LOCATION/BRAND...

SKU	DESCRIPTION	QUANTITY	LOCATION	COMMENTS

DATE:..../..../........   TIME......:........

COUNTED BY:...

LOCATION/BRAND...

SKU	DESCRIPTION	QUANTITY	LOCATION	COMMENTS

DATE:..../...../........ TIME......:.......

COUNTED BY:...

LOCATION/BRAND...

SKU	DESCRIPTION	QUANTITY	LOCATION	COMMENTS

DATE:..../...../.........   TIME......:.......

COUNTED BY:...

LOCATION/BRAND...

SKU	DESCRIPTION	QUANTITY	LOCATION	COMMENTS

DATE:..../...../.........   TIME......:........

COUNTED BY:...

LOCATION/BRAND...

SKU	DESCRIPTION	QUANTITY	LOCATION	COMMENTS

DATE:..../..../........   TIME......:........

COUNTED BY:..

LOCATION/BRAND..

SKU	DESCRIPTION	QUANTITY	LOCATION	COMMENTS

DATE:..../...../........   TIME......:.......

COUNTED BY:...

LOCATION/BRAND...

SKU	DESCRIPTION	QUANTITY	LOCATION	COMMENTS

DATE:..../...../......... TIME......:.......

COUNTED BY:...

LOCATION/BRAND...

SKU	DESCRIPTION	QUANTITY	LOCATION	COMMENTS

DATE:..../...../.........   TIME......:........

COUNTED BY:..

LOCATION/BRAND..

SKU	DESCRIPTION	QUANTITY	LOCATION	COMMENTS

DATE:..../...../........   TIME......:........
COUNTED BY:...
LOCATION/BRAND...

SKU	DESCRIPTION	QUANTITY	LOCATION	COMMENTS

DATE:..../...../........   TIME......:........

COUNTED BY:...

LOCATION/BRAND..

SKU	DESCRIPTION	QUANTITY	LOCATION	COMMENTS

Made in the USA
Las Vegas, NV
10 April 2024